W9-BAT-459

President and Cabinet

Katherine Krieg

rourkeeducationalmedia.com

Scan for Related Titles
and Teacher Resources

Before Reading:

Building Academic Vocabulary and Background Knowledge

Before reading a book, it is important to tap into what your child or students already know about the topic. This will help them develop their vocabulary, increase their reading comprehension, and make connections across the curriculum.

1. *Look at the cover of the book. What will this book be about?*
2. *What do you already know about the topic?*
3. *Let's study the Table of Contents. What will you learn about in the book's chapters?*
4. *What would you like to learn about this topic? Do you think you might learn about it from this book? Why or why not?*
5. *Use a reading journal to write about your knowledge of this topic. Record what you already know about the topic and what you hope to learn about the topic.*
6. *Read the book.*
7. *In your reading journal, record what you learned about the topic and your response to the book.*
8. *After reading the book complete the activities below.*

Content Area Vocabulary
Read the list. What do these words mean?

bill
capital
democracy
elect
expertise
override
policies
represents
resigns
term
veto

After Reading:

Comprehension and Extension Activity

After reading the book, work on the following questions with your child or students in order to check their level of reading comprehension and content mastery.

1. *Describe the commander-in-chief's job. (Summarize)*
2. *If the president's meeting with other world leaders does not go well, how would it affect the people of the United States? (Infer)*
3. *Why can a president only serve two terms? (Asking questions)*
4. *What are the criteria to become president? (Summarize)*
5. *What is the job of the Cabinet? (Summarize)*

Extension Activity

A new president was elected! Since times have changed a new Cabinet is needed and the president is taking suggestions from the American people. What should be the new Cabinet? How would this help the United States? What information can be obtained with this new Cabinet? Together with a classmate, write a proposal to submit to the newly elected president addressing ideas for your new Cabinet, why it is needed, the importance of the members, and what their duties would be.

Table of Contents

A Team

Do you know who the president is? The president is the leader of our country. It is the president's job to make important decisions about the United States of America.

As of 2013, there have been 44 presidents of the United States.

The president has many important responsibilities. It is too much for just one person to do everything. So, the president relies on the Cabinet to help. The Cabinet works with the president to make decisions.

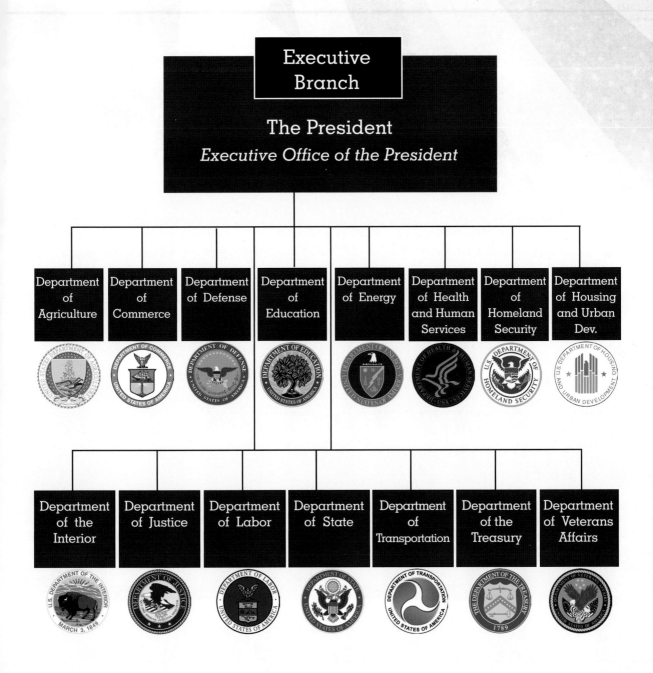

5

The president lives and works in the White House. The White House is in Washington, D.C., which is the **capital** of the country. The president's office there is called the Oval Office.

John Adams was the first president to live in the White House in 1800. In 1814, it was rebuilt after a fire destroyed it. There have been many changes to the White House since then.

The Cabinet works as a team with the president. It is made up of 15 people plus the vice president. The Cabinet meets with the president in the Cabinet Room. It is next to the Oval Office.

Each Cabinet member has an assigned seat in the Cabinet Room.

The president may hold private meetings in the Oval Office.

The President's Job

The president's role in the government is called the Executive Branch. The president is the leader of the American people. There are many jobs that only the president can do.

The first president of the United States was George Washington. (1732–1799)

The president must sign a **bill** in order for it to become a law. Or, the president can **veto** a bill. If a bill is vetoed, it can only become a law if Congress votes to **override** the president's decision.

George W. Bush
In office from 2001–2009

The president can decide whether or not to sign a bill.

The president is also the commander-in-chief of the armed forces. The president can send troops into battle, and make decisions about the country's defense.

Many presidents, including Abraham Lincoln, Jimmy Carter, and George W. Bush, served in the armed forces before their presidencies.

The armed forces help defend the country.

George H. W. Bush
In office from 1989–1993

The president is also the Chief Diplomat. It is the job of the president to meet with leaders of foreign countries to discuss decisions that may affect the United States.

The president also **represents** the country. The president often meets with leaders from other countries. It is the president's job to do what is best for the United States.

Electing a President

Not just anyone can become president. The president must be at least 35 years old, a U.S. citizen, and must have lived for at least 14 years in the United States.

A person is a U.S. citizen if he or she was born in the United States. You can also be a citizen if when you were born, your parents were citizens, even if they weren't living in the United States. A person who has moved to the United States can apply to become a U.S. citizen.

First-time voters must register to vote.

People over the age of 18 who are U.S. citizens can vote to **elect** the president. Elections for president are held every four years. They are always on the first Tuesday in November.

Whoever is elected will be president for one **term**. A term is four years long. Then, a new election will be held. If the president dies, **resigns**, or is removed from office during a term, the vice president becomes president.

Bill Clinton
In office from 1993–2001

Today, a person can serve up to two terms as president. But, originally, a president was allowed to serve any number of terms. In 1951, a law was passed to limit presidents to just two terms.

President Franklin Delano Roosevelt (1882–1945) was elected president four times. He was president from 1933 until he died in 1945.

The president is a very busy person. So, the president relies on the Cabinet to help with some of the work.

Each Cabinet member deals with a specific topic, such as education or transportation.

Cabinet members attend regular meetings.

The first Cabinet was created when George Washington was president. There were only four members.

Ronald Reagan
In office from 1981–1989

President Reagan holds a meeting in the Cabinet Room. The president always sits in the same chair at this table.

Fourteen of the Cabinet members are called secretaries. They are the leaders of their departments. The president gets to pick the Cabinet members.

The president asks the Cabinet for special reports about his or her area of **expertise**. The Cabinet also offers suggestions to the president for new **policies**.

The President's Cabinet

Department Seal	Cabinet Member	Responsibilities
	Secretary of State	Works with other countries.
	Secretary of the Treasury	Manages money.
	Secretary of Defense	Maintains armed forces.
	Attorney General	Deals with legal affairs and law enforcement.
	Secretary of Agriculture	Creates and enforces rules related to farming, forestry, and food.
	Secretary of Commerce	Promotes U.S. businesses.
	Secretary of Labor	Deals with U.S. jobs.

> The president meets with the Cabinet at least every other week.

Department Seal	Cabinet Member	Responsibilities
	Secretary of Health and Human Resources	Manages healthcare.
	Secretary of Housing and Development	Supports community development and home ownership.
	Secretary of the Department of the Interior	Oversees the use of land, including national park
	Secretary of Transportation	Deals with all issues related to transportation.
	Secretary of Energy	Maintains and develops energy resources.
	Secretary of Education	Promotes and manages education.
	Secretary of Veterans Affairs	Serves those who have been in the armed forces.
	Secretary of Homeland Security	Maintains terrorism awareness and coordinates response.

In the United States, people have the freedom to vote for a president they agree with. A president will pick Cabinet members who support these views. Voting makes **democracy** work.

President Obama selected his cabinet when he took office in 2009.

With the president and the Cabinet working together, they can get a lot accomplished. They keep the country running and are the faces of U.S. leadership to the rest of the world.

Glossary

bill (bil): a plan for a new law

capital (KAP-i-tuhl): the city in a country were the government works

democracy (di-MAH-kruh-see): a form of government in which people vote to choose their leaders

elect (i-LEKT): to pick a person by voting for him or her

expertise (EK-spurt-tees): knowledge or know-how

override (oh-vur-ride): to make ineffective

policies (PAH-li-sees): guidelines people use to help them take action

represents (rep-ri-ZENTS): to be a symbol of something

resigns (ri-ZINES): voluntarily leaves a job

term (turm): a period of time with a set limit

veto (VEE-toh): to reject a bill

Index

Show What You Know

1. What jobs does the president have?
2. How is the president elected? How often?
3. Why does the president need the Cabinet?
4. Who makes up the members of the Cabinet?
5. How are Cabinet members selected?

Websites to Visit

www.kids.nationalgeographic.com/kids/stories/peopleplaces/
  georgewashingtonicecream
www.mrnussbaum.com/presidents
www.ducksters.com/history/us_cabinet.php

About the Author

Katherine Krieg is the author of many books for young people. Katherine demonstrates her rights as a U.S. citizen by voting in every election.

Meet The Author!
www.meetREMauthors.com

www.rourkeeducationalmedia.com

PHOTO CREDITS: Cover/Title Page © Courtesy of U.S. Government; page 6 © Gary Blakeley; page 7 © Wikipedia, Charles Agholan; page 8, 15 © Library of Congress; page 9 © Charles Dharapak; page 10 © WilliamSherman; page 11 © George H.W. Bush Presidential Library and Museum; page 12 © Christopher Sutcher; page 13 © Steve Estvanik; page 14 © Visions of America LLC; page 16 © Nara; page 17 © U.S. National Archives and Records Administration; page 20 © Chuck Kennedy

Edited by: Jill Sherman

Cover by: Nicola Stratford, nicolastratford.com
Interior design by: Rhea Magaro

Library of Congress PCN Data

President and Cabinet/ Katherine Krieg
 (U.S. Government and Civics)
  ISBN 978-1-62717-678-1 (hard cover)
  ISBN 978-1-62717-800-6 (soft cover)
  ISBN 978-1-62717-916-4 (e-Book)
Library of Congress Control Number: 2014935453

Also Available as:

Printed in the United States of America, North Mankato, Minnesota